THE CAT

ELLA EARLE

summersdale

THE CAT

Summersdale Publishers Ltd
46 West Street
Chichester
West Sussex
PO19 1RP
UK

www.summersdale.com

Printed and bound in China

ISBN: 978-1-84953-142-9

Substantial discounts on bulk quantities of Summersdale books are available to corporations, professional associations and other organisations. For details telephone Summersdale Publishers on (+44-1243-771107), fax (+44-1243-786300) or email (nicky@summersdale.com).

To:..

From:..

In the beginning, God created man, but seeing him so feeble, He gave him the cat.

Warren Eckstein

It's really the cat's house – we just pay the mortgage.

Anonymous

You climb for the hell of it.

Edmund Hillary

The city of cats and the city of men exist one inside the other, but they are not the same city.

Italo Calvino

A cat pours his body on the floor like water. It is restful just to see him.

William Lyon Phelps

There are no grades of vanity, there are only grades of ability in concealing it.

Mark Twain

Cat's motto: No matter what you've done wrong, always try to make it look like the dog did it.

Anonymous

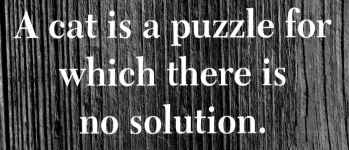

A cat is a puzzle for
which there is
no solution.

Hazel Nicholson

Cats are kindly masters,
just so long as you
remember your place.

Paul Gray

Life is like a tin of sardines. We are all looking for the key.

Alan Bennett

Contentment is, after all, simply refined indolence.

Thomas C. Haliburton

I have often wished I had time to cultivate modesty… But I am too busy thinking about myself.

Edith Sitwell

A cat improves the garden wall in sunshine, and the hearth in foul weather.

Judith Merkle Riley

There's no need for a piece of sculpture in a home that has a cat.

Wesley Bates

The cat has too much
spirit to have no heart.

Ernest Menaul

It's true hard work
never killed anybody,
but I figure, why take
the chance?

Ronald Reagan

God made the cat in order to give man the pleasure of caressing the tiger.

Anonymous

'You can't help that.
We're all mad here.'

The Cheshire Cat in
Alice in Wonderland **by Lewis Carroll**

You will always be lucky
if you know how to make
friends with strange cats.

Colonial American proverb

Kittens believe that all nature is occupied with their diversion.

François-Augustin de Paradis de Moncrif

Life is something that happens when you can't get to sleep.

Fran Lebowitz

Do not anticipate trouble or worry about what may never happen. Keep in the sunlight.

Benjamin Franklin

A cat is a lion in a jungle of small bushes.

Indian proverb

Our perfect companions
never have fewer
than four feet.

Colette

I believe cats to be
spirits come to earth.
A cat, I am sure, could
walk on a cloud without
coming through.

Jules Verne

Cats were put into the world to disprove the dogma that all things were created to serve man.

Paul Gray

Cats never strike a pose
that isn't photogenic.

Lilian Jackson Braun

Prowling his own quiet backyard or asleep by the fire, he is still only a whisker away from the wilds.

Jean Burden

Cats can work out mathematically the exact place to sit that will cause most inconvenience.

Pam Brown

A cat is more intelligent than people believe, and can be taught any crime.

Mark Twain

It is impossible to keep
a straight face in the
presence of one
or more kittens.

Cynthia E. Varnado

Attitude is a little thing that makes a big difference.

Winston Churchill

I love cats because I enjoy my home; and little by little, they become its visible soul.

Jean Cocteau

In ancient times cats were worshipped as gods; they have not forgotten this.

Terry Pratchett

Whosoever is delighted in solitude is either wild beast or god.

Francis Bacon

Animals are such agreeable friends – they ask no questions, they pass no criticisms.

George Eliot

Often the best way to overcome desire is to satisfy it.

W. Somerset Maugham

Cats seem to go on the principle that it never does any harm to ask for what you want.

Joseph Wood Krutch

The dream of a cat is filled with mice.

Arab proverb

Freedom lies in being bold.

Robert Frost

If I only had a little humility, I'd be perfect.

Ted Turner

...if you tell me that curiosity killed the cat, I say only the cat died nobly.

Arnold Edinborough

I named my kitten Rose
– fur soft as a petal,
claws sharper
than thorns.

Astrid Alauda

As every cat owner knows, nobody owns a cat.

Ellen Perry Berkeley

Happy is the home with at least one cat.

Italian proverb

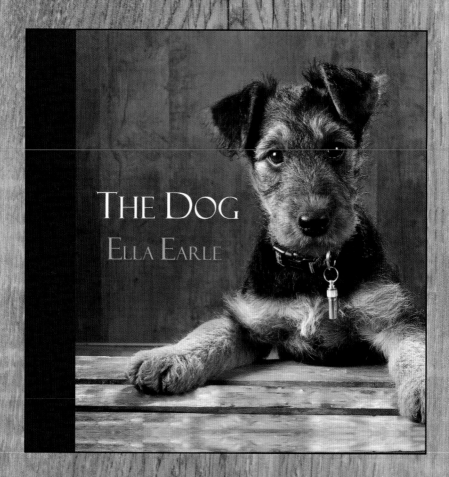

THE DOG

ELLA EARLE

THE DOG

ELLA EARLE

ISBN: 978-1-84953-143-6   Hardback   £6.99

*Histories are more full of examples
of the fidelity of dogs than of friends.*

Alexander Pope

Combining lavish and amusing photographs
with whimsical and thoughtful quotations, this
charming celebration of canine companions is a
must-have for all dog lovers.